Good Morning Mothers

A Mourning Mother's Devotional to Healing

Sabrina Young

ZYIA CONSULTING
Illuminate & Transcend

Good Morning Mothers: A Mourning Mother's Devotional to Healing

Copyright © 2022 by Sabrina Young

ZYIA CONSULTING
Illuminate & Transcend

Zyia Consulting
Book Writing & Publishing Company
www.nyishaddavis.com
nyisha.d.davis@gmail.com

Unless otherwise noted, all Scripture quotations are taken from www.blueletterbible.org.

Cover Design: Zyia Consulting

ISBN: 978-0-578-38647-8

Printed in the United States of America.

Dedication

To the Mothers who are willing to face and fight
through life encounters.

Content

1 Peter 5:7

Casting all your care upon him; for he careth for you.

Not only does God love us, He cares. He attends to us as we attend to our earthly children. As we care for them, He asks us to put them and all of our cares upon Him, because of His heart for us.

Mothers, let God take care of you and your cares today.

Hebrews 12:1

Wherefore seeing we also are compassed about with so great a cloud of witnesses, let us lay aside every weight, and the sin which doth so easily beset us, and let us run with patience the race that is set before us,

As mothers, we go through so much in life, and have to take on so much. Our daily life encounters consist of dealing with the issues and problems of our children, work, school, church and more. It is easy for us to get agitated, which may cause us to easily become angry, snap, and tell someone off. We feel like the weight of the world is on our shoulders. A lot of the time, the enemy will use people that are closest to us to cause us to slip to do or say a bad thing. However, we must remember to apply the fruits of the spirit to each and every situation to run this race called life.

Mothers, through it all, we must let patience have it's works in us!

Nehemiah 8:10

Then he said unto them, Go your way, eat the fat, and drink the sweet, and send portions unto them for whom nothing is prepared: for this day is holy unto our Lord: neither be ye sorry; for the joy of the LORD is your strength.

Oftentimes, we allow things to trouble our spirit so bad we won't eat, sleep or drink. Nehemiah reminds us that not only should we eat and not be sorry, but to remember those who have nothing prepared. I want to encourage us, as mothers, to remember another mother today who is stressed, going through it, or just a single mom. When you prepare a meal for yourself, cook enough for the neighbor who is a single mother. You will find joy in this, even on your worse day.

This will bring joy to them, and this pleases God. Where there is God, there is joy and strength! Build yourself today.

Eat or feed another Mother today!

Psalms 56:8

Thou tellest my wanderings: put thou my
tears into thy bottle: are they
not in thy book?

God has a record of every tear we cry and everything we do. None of our tears are for waste. God sees and knows our pain. He is keeping track of our tears and pain. They mean that much to Him. Mothers, our tears matter to God.

Your pain is not in vain.

Philippians 4:4

Rejoice in the Lord always: and again
I say, Rejoice.

The word "rejoice" has always stood out to me in this scripture. The Apostle Paul reminds us to continue to rejoice. But, he said in the Lord. This lets me know that, even in our sorrows, as long as we are in the Lord, we can always find some way to rejoice.

Mothers, stay in the Lord, and keep rejoicing through it all!

Philippians 4:7

And the peace of God, which passeth all understanding, shall keep your hearts and minds through Christ Jesus.

God will allow you to be in a peaceful state that you won't understand in times when you feel like you should be upset, confused, lost or worried. Through His son, Jesus, He will allow His peace to rest upon you. Your heart will not hurt, and your mind will not wonder so much.

May His peace rest upon you today.

Psalms 30:5

For his anger endureth but a moment; in his favour is life: weeping may endure for a night, but joy cometh in the morning.

Your morning does not have to relate to a time of day. It can be a set time when you find some type of joy in your situation. Rather it is birthing a ministry from your pain, being able to reflect on good memories as a mother, or completing counseling sessions, courses, or any obstacles that tried to hinder you from functioning or moving forward in life after the loss, situation or circumstance. It's ok to cry, Mother. But, remember that your morning is approaching.

Wake up to it.

Exodus 14:14

The LORD shall fight for you, and ye shall
hold your peace.

If you keep a hold of your peace and do not let situations and circumstances cause you to let it go, He will fight the enemy for you. But, if you let go of your peace, and allow people, places and circumstances take you out of a peaceful state, then He won't fight for you.

Keep a tight grip on your peace, and let God fight for you!

Mark 11:25

And when ye stand praying, forgive, if ye have ought against any: that your Father also which is in heaven may forgive you your trespasses.

To get forgiveness, we have to forgive. We must first forgive ourselves for any faults that we feel we have afflicted upon ourselves, then others. We can't forgive others and not forgive ourselves. If we do not forgive ourselves, then we would remain in a complacent place of unforgiveness. Most of all, we will hinder our blessings by not forgiving others. The scripture clearly says in order for God to forgive us, we must forgive others. So, before we can move on asking anything of God, we must have a clean slate by forgiving others of their wrongdoings, as well as ourselves. As of this day, Mother, set yourself and others free.

Forgive and live!

Psalms 34:18

The LORD is nigh unto them that are of a broken heart; and saveth such as be of a contrite spirit.

Please know that you are not alone. God is close to you. He's near and knows this situation has broken your heart and caused your spirit to be crushed. He is there to save you. He will not allow you to drown or perish. Feel the Lord's presence.

Put your hand in His, and let Him save you even in this.

Psalms 73:26

My flesh and my heart faileth: but God is
the strength of my heart, and
my portion for ever.

Because of the flesh, we allow the issues of life to come in, and sometimes change our hearts towards people, places and things. We allow the issues of life to affect us; how we treat people, what we say, and how we feel. David reminds us that God is the strength of our hearts. He is who will cause us to treat people right, even when they have wronged us.

Today, let God in to help you love in spite of!

Matthew 5:4

Blessed are they that mourn: for they shall be comforted.

Sometimes we feel cursed, forgotten and abandoned, because of certain things we have encountered in life. But, this scripture reminds us that we are blessed and that God, through His Holy Spirit, comforts us in the time of mourning.

Mothers, remember, on this day, you are blessed and not cursed, comforted, and not left alone.

John 16:22

And ye now therefore have sorrow: but I will see you again, and your heart shall rejoice, and your joy no man taketh from you.

It may hurt now. You may not understand it. But, know God is not going to leave you in this state. He is coming to revisit the situation. No one will be able to make you cry or feel bad about the same thing again.

Mothers, you will find joy even in this.

Matthew 11:28

Come unto me, all ye that labour and are heavy laden, and I will give you rest.

It's ok to take a day off. Turn off the phone, find a sitter for the children, take a mini-vacay, or just take a day to rest in God's arm; just you and Him. We will crash if we don't. Take a load off, read a book, and stay in bed.

Please, Mother, get some rest.

Matthew 11:29

Take my yoke upon you, and learn of me;
for I am meek and lowly in heart: and ye
shall find rest unto your souls.

One of the reasons things are so heavy, is simply because we take on things and assignments God has not designed for us. For this reason, we are overwhelmed, weighed down, and feel heavily burdened. Seek God for guidance. Study the word that you may hear from Him.

Just because we are doing a good thing, does not mean we are doing a God thing.

Matthew 11:30

For my yoke is easy, and my
burden is light.

We like to say, "Just because it's hard does not mean it's not God." We have to discern when it's not God. When it feels unbearable and overwhelming, ask yourself, "Is this God?" We must continue in our personal relationship and daily conversations with Him. In this, you will be able to distinguish betwen His voice and discern His tests.

If it's heavy and hard, it might not be God!

Joshua 1:9

Have not I commanded thee? Be strong and of a good courage; be not afraid, neither be thou dismayed: for the LORD thy God is with thee whithersoever thou goest.

God did not just make a statement, He made a commandment; be strong and courageous. Just like a commander in the army, we must obey Him, knowing that He has the instructions to lead and guide us. Move forward. Do whatever is necessary, in this season, to get through this tough time. Get to the other side of it, knowing that our Father in Heaven is there with you. There is no need to be afraid. Go where you need to go. Do what you need to do.

God is with you!

John 14:27

Peace I leave with you, my peace I give unto you: not as the world giveth, give I unto you. Let not your heart be troubled, neither let it be afraid.

Some of us find peace in financial gain, materialistic things, or in certain people. When we don't have or lose them we lose our peace. During those times, we pick up the spirit of fear, because of the thoughts of being talked about, viewed a certain way, or the thought of being lonely troubles our heart. Why is it that we search for something we already have? This could be the reason our hearts are so troubled. I encourage you today to look at and thank God for what and who you have, verses what and who you want. So what, if they walk away. So what, if you ain't got a pocket full of money. God will supply all your needs. It's not always about what you want. Think about what you have.

Your peace has been there the whole time.

James 1:2

My brethren, count it all joy when ye fall into divers tempations;

God is not saying that we should rejoice
in our shortcomings. He is saying have
joy, knowing that His word covers us
even when we fall; Jesus allowed grace to
come about. He knew we would fall. But,
because of Him, we cannot fail. Get up!
Smile! Get back in the race!

It was only a test...

James 1:3

Knowing this, that the trying of your faith worketh patience.

In this scripture, James simply talks about the trials of life when he states the trying of your faith; the things that irritate us and our tribulations. God wants us better and to mature in Him, so He can trust us to be strong solid servants. God doesn't allow these things to hurt us, only to help us. It's not the trial that's trying you, it's the patience that's working!

Let it work!

Matthew 19:14

But Jesus said, Suffer little children, and forbid them not, to come unto me: for of such is the kingdom of heaven.

It is a mother's instinct to hold their child close to them. It's amazing how children can have more faith than their parents. When it's time, they go off to school, get a mate, move out, have life challenges, and keep moving. The child is, at times, stronger than the parent. As parents, we tend to feel a void of our child no longer being in our presence. We get sad, upset, resentful, all the above. God is saying do not keep the children from going or coming. He has their back. There is no need to worry. They belong to Him. The kingdom belongs to them.

To inherit the kingdom, we all must be like the children.

Psalms 127:3

Lo, children are an heritage of the LORD:
and the fruit of the womb is his reward.

God never said what particular child comes from Him. He said children, period. Stop second guessing the child you had out of wedlock or the child you had that you thought was a mistake. That child...came from God Himself. If God didn't want you to have him/her, they wouldn't be here. That child is a benefit to you, not a burden.

Thank God for your inheritance!

Psalms 147:3

He healeth the broken in heart, and
bindeth up their wounds.

Your heart may be broken right now, but know healing is your portion. Dr. Jesus is there to see about you. You may be in the waiting room, but He will not let you leave without taking care of your wounds.

Jesus, He will fix it!

Psalms 9:9

The LORD also will be a refuge for the oppressed, a refuge in times of trouble.

Know that you are safe in God. You are safe, because you are in Him. When you are sad, and life issues form against you, you are safe in Him. Rest in Him.

You are safe.

Psalms 90:14

O satisfy us early with thy mercy; that we may rejoice and be glad all our days.

When the Lord continues to wake us up each day, He is giving us a daily reminder of how much He loves us. At times, as mothers, we feel unloved because of the way we love and nurture. For some reason, we never feel the same measure we give out. If we can just recognize that just because God woke us up, somebody loves us. And, that somebody is Him.

Now, rejoice and be glad!

Psalms 118:24

This is the day which the LORD hath made;
we will rejoice and be glad in it.

Have you included the Lord in this day? Or is it full of everything you want or what you want to do? You didn't make this day. Rejoice! He chose you to be in it, so add Him in it.

He is the Creator of it.

Isaiah 26:3

Thou wilt keep him in perfect peace,
whose mind is stayed on thee: because
he trusteth in thee.

It's amazing how we search for, pray for, cry for, and try to find peace. Especially, as mothers. We remind the ones we believe are disturbing our peace about how much we want it, and how much their disturbing it. If it takes everything in us, we are going to find it. Most of the time, we allow our minds to become cluttered by allowing so much to occupy it. We disturb our own peace.

We have to keep our minds on God.

Ephesians 6:10

Finally, my brethren, be strong in the Lord, and in the power of his might.

Stop trying to find strength in that bottle, that smoke, that person, or anything besides the Lord. Anything or anyone that is not of or in the Lord is subject to make you weak. You should not even receive advice from someone who does not encourage you in the Lord.

Yes, you need strength to be strong, but don't forget to pray for might!

Job 38:12

Hast thou commanded the morning since
thy days; and caused the day spring
to know his place;

Command your day. Tell your day what it's going to be. Speak to it. It belongs to you. God gave it to you. Tell it that it will not be sorrowful, but joyful; blessed and not cursed. It is what you say that it will be.

Determine your day.

Lamentations 3:23

They are new every morning: great is
thy faithfulness.

As each day approaches, God gives us newness; new grace and new mercy. He is so faithful to us. We do not have to operate or function in life with what is old. Just because you don't cry like you use to, does not mean you still don't hurt. Just because you walked away from that person, does not mean you still don't care. Just because you left that job, does not mean you don't want income. This morning is fresh and new. Embrace it! Get rid of the old.

Walk into the new.

Healing is Your Portion